ADORABLE ANIMAL FRIENDSHIPS

By Virginia Loh-Hagan

Disclaimer: This series focuses on the strangest of the strange. Have fun reading about strange people and things! But please do not try any of the antics in this book. Be safe and smart!

45th Parallel Press

Published in the United States of America by Cherry Lake Publishing
Ann Arbor, Michigan
www.cherrylakepublishing.com

Reading Adviser: Marla Conn MS, Ed., Literacy specialist, Read-Ability, Inc.
Book Designer: Melinda Millward

Photo Credits: © Noah's Ark Animal Sanctuary, cover, 20, 21; © Zanna Holstova / Shutterstock.com, 1; © enciktat / Shutterstock.com, 5; © Greg Kushmerek / Shutterstock.com, 6; © Dixi_ / iStock.com, 7; © Cristian Gusa / Shutterstock.com, 8; © SABANCANPHOTOGRAPHY / Shutterstock.com, 9; © RollingEarth / iStock.com, 10; © nattanan726 / Shutterstock.com, 11; © justhavealook / iStock.com, 12; © Frankix / iStock.com, 14; © Karel Gallas / Shutterstock.com, 15; © Lightofchairat / Dreamstime.com, 16; © ASSOCIATED PRESS / apimages.com, 17; © Marni Rae Photography / Shutterstock.com, 18; © Nonchanon / Shutterstock.com, 19; © Barcroft Media / Gettyimages.com, 22; © K.A.Willis / Shutterstock.com, 24; © Holger Ehlers / Alamy Stock Photo, 25; © Lee Torrens / Shutterstock.com, 26; © taviphoto / Shutterstock.com, 28; © Zanna Holstova / Shutterstock.com, 29; © AtiwatPhotography / Shutterstock.com, 30; © Koichi Kamoshida / Gettyimages.com, 31

45th Parallel Press is an imprint of Cherry Lake Publishing.

Library of Congress Cataloging-in-Publication Data

Names: Loh-Hagan, Virginia, author.
Title: Adorable animal friendships / by Virginia Loh-Hagan.
Description: Ann Arbor : Cherry Lake Publishing, [2018] | Series: Stranger than fiction |
    Audience: Grade 4 to 6. | Includes bibliographical references and index.
Identifiers: LCCN 2017031233| ISBN 9781534107601 (hardcover) | ISBN 9781534108592 (pbk) |
    ISBN 9781534109582 (pdf) | ISBN 9781534120570 (hosted ebook)
Subjects: LCSH: Social behavior in animals—Juvenile literature. | Friendship—Juvenile literature. |
    Animal behavior—Juvenile literature.
Classification: LCC QL775 .L64 2018 | DDC 591.56—dc23
LC record available at https://lccn.loc.gov/2017031233

Printed in the United States of America
Corporate Graphics

About the Author

Dr. Virginia Loh-Hagan is an author, university professor, former classroom teacher, and curriculum designer. Her dogs, Woody and Dotty, are the best of friends! She lives in San Diego with her very tall husband and very naughty dogs. To learn more about her, visit www.virginialoh.com.

Table of Contents

Introduction

Animals are part of a food chain. Predators are hunters. They eat prey. Prey are hunted as food. Predators and prey shouldn't be friends. But some are. Some animals form unlikely friendships.

Interspecies friendships are bonds formed between animals of different species. Species are animal types. It's cute to see animals play. It's even cuter to see animals play with different animals.

But there are strange friendships. And then there are really strange friendships. Some animal friendships are really strange. They're animal odd couples. They're so strange that they're hard to believe. They sound like fiction. But these stories are all true!

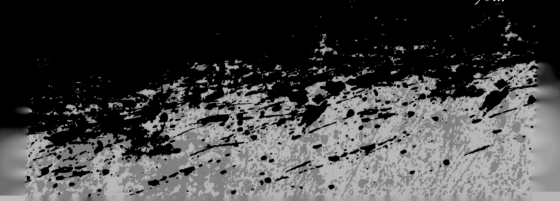

Imagine being friends with someone who wants to eat you.

chapter one

Dog and Lion

Milo is a dachshund. He is 11 pounds (5 kilograms). Bonedigger is a lion. He is 500 pounds (227 kg). Milo and Bonedigger do everything together. They live in a wildlife park in Oklahoma.

Bonedigger has a bone sickness. He is disabled. Disabled means not being able to move well. Milo took care of him when he was a lion cub. Cubs are baby animals. Milo comforted him. He protected him.

Milo and Bonedigger hug. They eat raw meat together. They play together. Milo

Dachshunds are called weiner dogs.

tries to copy Bonedigger when he growls. Lions growl to talk to other lions.

chapter two

Cat and Crow

Cassie is a cat. She lives in Massachusetts. She showed up at Wally and Ann Collito's house in 1999. She was a **stray** kitten. Stray means not having a home or family. Cassie let the Collitos feed her. But she also let a crow feed her.

Moses was a crow. He fed Cassie worms and bugs. He protected her from other animals. He **cawed** when Cassie went toward the street. Caws are the sounds crows make. He pecked on the door for Cassie every morning.

Moses and Cassie hung out together all the time. This lasted for 5 years.

American crows live only 7 to 8 years in the wild.

Then Moses stopped showing up. The Collitos think he died. Cats usually live longer than crows.

chapter three

Tiger Cubs and Chimpanzee

Mitra and Shiva are white tiger cubs. They were born during **Hurricane** Hanna. Hurricanes are bad storms. Hurricane Hanna was the deadliest storm in 2008. It hit the East Coast.

The tiger cubs were living in a wildlife park in South Carolina. The park flooded. The cubs had to be moved. Their mother was **stressed**. Stressed means tense and worried. This made the mother dangerous.

The tiger cubs were taken to a warmer and dryer place. Zookeeper China York took care of the cubs. But she had help.

The tiger cubs came from Doc Antle's park.

Anjana is a chimpanzee. She helped take care of the tiger cubs.

Anjana acted like the cubs' mother. Sometimes, the cubs would cry. Anjana gave them her fingers to suck on. She was gentle with them. She kept them happy. She gave them bottles of milk. She cleaned them with wipes. She played with them. She tumbled with them. She petted them. She took care of them until the cubs got too big.

Anjana learned from York. She has a strong friendship with York. York raised Anjana. Anjana copied how York cares for animals. Anjana especially likes big cats. She's taken care of a baby puma. She's taken care of a leopard. She's taken care of lion cubs.

Chimpanzees are part of the great ape family. They're not monkeys.

Explained by Science

Biologists say relationships are formed to reach a specific goal. Interspecies friendships happen in three types of animals. They happen among younger animals. These animals need protection. They need care. Interspecies friendships happen among animals living in captivity. Captivity means not living in the wild. People take care of captive animals. Interspecies friendships also happen among stressed animals. These animals need other animals. Clive Wynne is a university professor. He says these friendships aren't about animal behavior. He thinks they're more about human impact on nature.

chapter four

Elephant and Sheep

Themba was an elephant. His mother fell off a cliff. She died. Themba was 6 months old. He was alone. People saved him. They took him to a wildlife park in South Africa.

Albert is a sheep. He was put in Themba's pen. He kept Themba company. At first, Themba didn't like Albert. He chased him out. Albert hid. Themba used his trunk to touch Albert. Albert got bored of hiding. They soon became

friends. They walked together. They took dust baths together. They slept together. Themba rested his trunk on Albert's back. Albert copied Themba. He ate the same thing Themba did.

A baby elephant is called a calf.

chapter five

Hippo and Tortoise

A storm hit the coast of Kenya, Africa. This happened in 2004. Owen is a hippo. He was a baby at that time. He lost his **herd**. Herds are animal groups. Owen was stranded on a coral reef. People saved him. They took him to a wildlife park.

Owen was scared. He was confused. He hid behind Mzee. Mzee is a tortoise. He was 130 years old. He didn't like Owen at first. But they soon became best friends. They lived together. They ate together. They slept together. They **wallowed** together. Wallow means to make and sit in a mud hole. This is how hippos cool off.

The tortoise's shape and color look like a hippo.

chapter six

Giraffe and Ostrich

Bea is a giraffe. Wilma is an ostrich. They live in Busch Gardens in Florida. They live in a special park. This park has a lot of African animals. Bea and Wilma were both born there. They both have long necks. They're best friends.

Wilma is 7 years older than Bea. But age doesn't matter to them. They like each other's company. They live on 65 acres (26 hectares). They can choose to be apart. They can choose to be with their own kind. Yet they're always together.

Giraffes and ostriches are both curious animals.

Bea likes to use her tongue. She explores everything, even Wilma. Wilma doesn't mind.

chapter seven

Bear, Lion, and Tiger

Police raided a house in Atlanta, Georgia. They did this in 2001. They were looking for drugs. They looked in the basement. They found three animal cubs. Leo is a lion. Baloo is a black bear. Shere Khan is a tiger. The drug dealer kept them as pets.

The cubs were sick. They were starving. Their cage was dirty. They were hugging each other. They were moved to a wildlife park in Georgia. They healed there. Baloo was hurt the most. The drug dealer kept ropes around him. The ropes were tight. His skin grew around the ropes.

People should not keep wild animals as pets.

Baloo went to the hospital. That was the only time the cubs were apart. Shere Khan and Leo were upset. They paced. They cried. Baloo returned to them. The three animals were together for 15 years.

People called them the "BLT." The animals were always together. They loved each other. They nuzzled. They rubbed heads. They played.

Leo got sick. He died. Shere Khan and Baloo were sad. They were with him during his last days. They had their chance to say goodbye.

The park made a statue of Leo.

Spotlight Biography

"Doc" Antle lives in Myrtle Beach, South Carolina. He's the founder and director of TIGERS. TIGERS stands for The Institute for Greatly Endangered and Rare Species. Antle has a private wildlife park. He takes care of animals. He breeds animals. He trains animals. He lives with his animals. His park is 50 acres (20 hectares). It's the "greatest hands-on animal experience in the world." It has a lot of animal friendships. Antle's first animal friendship was a tiger cub and Antle's pet dog. He makes a lot of videos. He does a lot of TV shows. He advises moviemakers. He's an expert on animals. He says, "I'm unbelievably lucky. If there is a charmed life, I've already led four of them."

chapter eight

Kangaroo and Wombat

Anzac is a kangaroo. When he was a baby, he was **abandoned**. Abandoned means being left behind. Anzac's mother was hit by a car. She died. Anzac was in her pouch. That's how he survived.

Anzac was 5 months old. Usually, baby kangaroos stay in their mothers' pouches for 8 months. Anzac was too young to be on his own. He was saved. He was taken to a wildlife park in Australia.

The animal keepers made a pouch. They put Anzac in a pouch with Peggy. Peggy is

A baby kangaroo is called a joey.

a wombat. She was 5 months old. She was abandoned. Her mother was also hit by a car and died.

Peggy and Anzac were both orphans. Orphans are children without families. They were lonely. They slept together. They comforted each other. They felt each other's movements. They felt each other's heartbeats. They touched noses. They sucked each other's ears. They groomed each other. Groom means to clean.

They also acted the same. They were both social. They both had a lot of energy. They were both playful.

They both eat plants. They don't eat meat. This means they won't be a threat to each other. Threat means danger. Anzac and Peggy won't eat each other.

Kangaroos and wombats are night animals. That's why they get hit by cars. Drivers can't see as well at night.

26

Try This!

- Visit a zoo. Or visit a wildlife center. Learn about food chains. Think about what each animal eats. Think about what eats them.

- Watch online videos about animal friendships. Rank the videos. Find the top three cutest animal friendships.

- Watch two animals together. Study how they act around each other. Are they playing, or are they hunting?

- Make a new friend. Be friends with someone who is not like you. Do something that you normally wouldn't do.

- Imagine your own animal friendship. Which two animals would you like to see be friends?

- Go to an animal shelter. Help take care of the animals. Help find them homes.

chapter nine

Puppies and Chicken

Mabel was a chicken. She was 1 year old. A horse stepped on her foot. Mabel's foot was broken. She was moved into her owners' home. Her owners were Edward and Ros Tate. They live on a farm in England.

The Tates had a dog. The dog was named Nettle. Nettle had just had puppies. Nettle would rather go outside than watch her puppies. So, Mabel watched the puppies for her.

Mabel kept the puppies warm. She snuggled next to them. She **roosted** on them. Roosting means sitting or resting.

The Tates were going to cook Mabel. But they changed their minds.

Tate said, "She took to them like they were her own chicks."
Chicks are baby chickens.

chapter ten

Snake and Hamster

There's a zoo in Tokyo, Japan. A snake named Aochan lives there. He's a rat snake. He's 3 feet (91.4 centimeters) long. He stopped eating frozen rats. Zookeepers put a hamster in his cage. They thought Aochan would eat it. But he didn't. He left it alone.

The hamster was 3.5 inches (9 cm) long. He wasn't afraid of Aochan. He often slept on top of Aochan. Zookeepers named the hamster Gohan. Gohan means meal in Japanese. He was believed to be lucky.

Zookeepers thought something was wrong with Aochan. But Aochan was

In many countries, it's illegal to feed live animals to other animals.

fine. He just wanted a friend. The two were friends for several months. Then zookeepers moved Gohan to his own cage. Just to be safe.

Consider This!

Take a Position! Some zookeepers think animals should share the same space. Do you think predators and prey should live together in zoos? Or do you think animals should have their own areas? Argue your point with reasons and evidence.

Say What? Do some research. Find another strange animal friendship. Describe the friendship. Explain why the friendship is strange.

Think About It! "Opposites attract." This is a popular saying. Think about your own friendships. Are you friends with someone who is not like you? Describe your friendship. Explain why you two are friends.

Learn More!

- Holland, Jennifer S. *The Dog and the Piglet: And Four Other Stories of Animal Friendships.* New York: Workman Publishing Company, 2012.
- Quattlebaum, Mary. *Together Forever! True Stories of Amazing Animal Friendships.* Washington, DC: National Geographic, 2016.
- Spelman, Lucy. *National Geographic Animal Encyclopedia: 2,500 Animals with Photos, Maps, and More!* Washington, DC: National Geographic, 2012.

Glossary

abandoned (uh-BAN-duhnd) left behind

cawed (KAWD) made a sound that a crow makes

chicks (CHIKS) baby chickens

cub (KUHB) baby animal

groomed (GROOMD) cleaned

herd (HURD) an animal group

hurricane (HUR-ih-kane) bad storm

interspecies (IN-tur-spee-sheez) animals from different species

orphans (OR-fuhnz) children without parents

predators (PRED-uh-turz) hunters

prey (PRAY) animals hunted as food

roosted (ROOST-id) sat or rested

species (SPEE-sheez) groups or types of animals

stray (STRAY) not having a home or family

stressed (STRESD) overly worried and tense

threat (THRET) danger

wallowed (WAH-lohd) made a hole in mud and hung out in it to cool off

Index